This Coupon Notebook
Belongs To:

www.ingramcontent.com/pod-product-compliance
Lightning Source LLC
Chambersburg PA
CBHW070428220526
45466CB00004B/1584
9781655812422